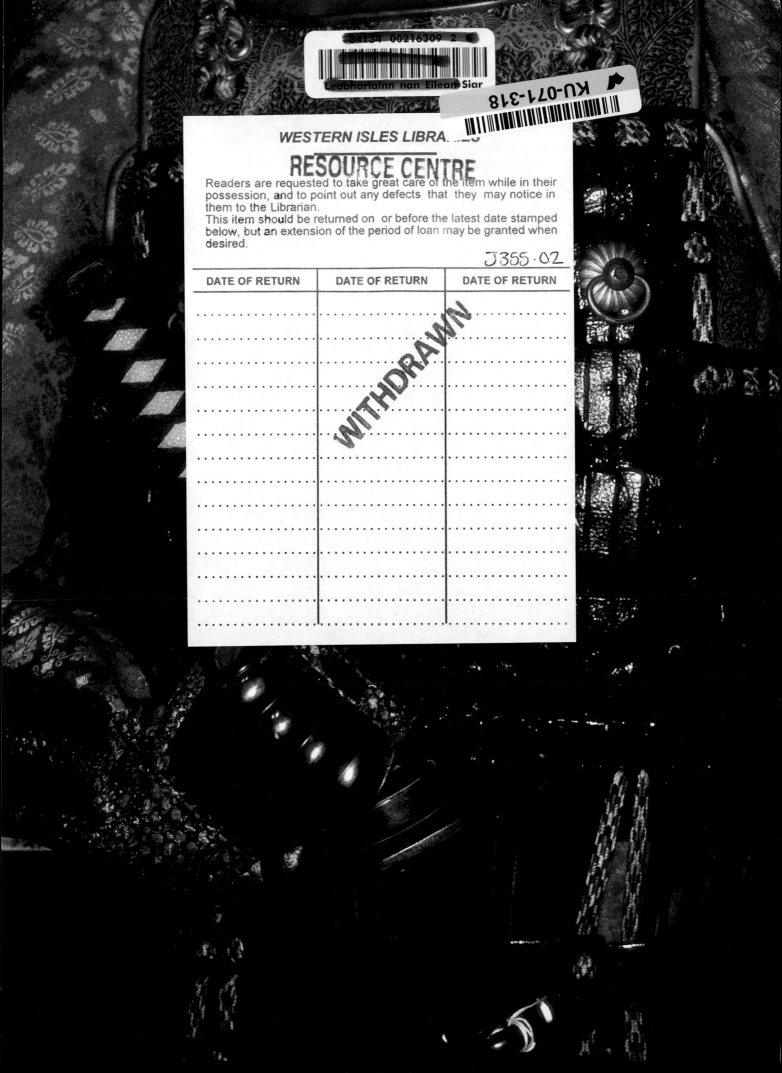

RESOURCE CENTRE

RESOURCE CENTRE

CONTENTS

Author and artist:
Mark Bergin studied at Eastbourne College of Art and has specialised in historical reconstructions, aviation and maritime subjects for over 20 years. He lives in Bexhill-on-Sea with his wife and three children.

Historical consultant:
Andrew Robertshaw taught history before joining the National Army Museum, Chelsea, in 1984. He is currently responsible for the Museum's education services. He is also an author, military historian and battlefield guide. He lives in Surrey with his wife and daughter.

Additional artists: **Gerald Wood, Ray and Corinne Burrows, Tony Townsend, John James**

Series creator and designer: **David Salariya**
Editor: **Karen Barker Smith**
Assistant Editor: **Michael Ford**

With thanks to Mark and David at The Lanes Armoury.
www.thelanesarmoury.co.uk

Published in Great Britain in 2003 by
Book House, an imprint of
The Salariya Book Company Ltd
25 Marlborough Place, Brighton BN1 1UB

Please visit the Salariya Book Company at:
www.salariya.com
www.book-house.co.uk

ISBN 1 904194 76 1

A catalogue record for this book is available from the British Library.

Printed and bound in Belgium.
Printed on paper from sustainable forests.

Photographic credits
t=top b=bottom c=centre l=left r=right

The Art Archive/ Belvoir Castle/ Eileen Tweedy: 34/35t
The Art Archive/ Eileen Tweedy: 18/19, 34b
The Art Archive/ JFB: 17r
The Art Archive/ Harper Collins Publishers: 30
The Art Archive/ Musée des Beaux Art Nantes/ Dagli Orti: 20 bl
The Art Archive/ Musée du Château de Versailles/ Dagli Orti: 28bl
The Art Archive/ National Archives Washington DC: 38tr, 39c
The Art Archive/ Wellington Museum, London/ Eileen Tweedy: 31tl
Ashmolean Museum, Oxford, UK/ The Bridgeman Art Library: 15br
Breslich and Foss: 22r, 23l, 33l, 36l, 37r, 41l
Bridgeman Art Library: 12/13, 25tl
Cheltenham Art Gallery and Museum, Gloucestershire, UK/ The Giraudon/ The Bridgeman Art Library: 25tr
Kunsthistorisches Museum, Vienna, Austria/ The Bridgeman Art Library: 10tl
Mountain High Maps/ copyright 1993 Digital Wisdom Inc: 6/7c, 8tl, 10r, 12tl, 13tl, 16tl, 18tr, 20tl, 22tr, 26tl, 30tr, 36tl
Nigel Hillyard of The Sealed Knot: 14l, 15tl
Smith Art Gallery and Museum, Stirling, Scotland/ The Bridgeman Art Library: 19tr
Victoria and Albert Museum, London, UK/ The Bridgeman Art Library: 21tl

©The Salariya Book Company: 1, 2/3, 5, 9, 11br, 13t, 19tl, 22bc, 27tr, 27l, 29r, 31tr, 31r, 35bl, 37cl, 37b, 40tr, 41bl, 46/47, 48

Every effort has been made to trace copyright holders. The Salariya Book Company apologises for any unintentional omissions and would be pleased, in such cases, to add an acknowledgement in future editions.

Warfare in the 16th to 19th Centuries

Written and illustrated by
Mark Bergin

BOOK HOUSE

OVERVIEW

$\mathcal{B}$etween the 16th and 19th centuries many conflicts were fought around the globe. These were partly due to the ideologies and expansionist policies of countries and their rulers. Over this period military strategies and fighting techniques changed dramatically with the use of new weapons such as gunpowder. By mobilising strong armies and navies to control more of the world's surface, European powers sought to build vast empires in the 16th and 17th centuries. Many of the wars in the following period saw those empires crumbling as occupied territories fought back.

ARMADA, 1588
In 1588 King Philip II of Spain sent a large invasion fleet to attack Elizabeth I's England. This was successfully fought off by a smaller fleet led by Sir Francis Drake.

REVOLUTIONARY WAR
Although Britain's armed forces were among the best in the world, the American colonies rebelled in 1775 to claim their freedom. They were helped by Britain's old enemies, the French and Spanish.

US CIVIL WAR
The American Civil War (1861-1865) was one of the most significant events in the history of the United States. Three million men fought on both sides in the conflict. Northern (Union) states and southern (Confederate) states fought each other over whether the national government or individual states should govern them.

NORTH AMERICA

EUROPE

Atlantic Ocean

AFRICA

Pacific Ocean

SOUTH AMERICA

INDIAN WARS
North American Indians fought many battles with new settlers who colonised their land. The new settlers brought diseases, put up boundaries on native hunting grounds and slaughtered the buffalo herds. By the 1860s the US government had moved many tribes to reservations, but many chose to fight against such oppression.

ENGLISH CIVIL WAR
King Charles I and Parliament fought over the power to govern the country between 1642 and 1643. The country was divided in its support for either side.

JACOBITE REBELLION
In 1745 an uprising was led in Scotland by Prince Charles Stuart. He sailed from France and united various clan chieftains in order to take the crown of England from King George II.

FREDERICK THE GREAT
Frederick (ruled 1740-1786) was king of Prussia (present-day northern Germany). He increased Prussia's territory and influence by campaigning against his neighbours in the Seven Years' War.

RUSSIA

JAPAN

CRIMEAN WAR
The war was caused by a dispute between Russia, France and the Ottoman Empire over rights of protection of Christian shrines in Ottoman-controlled holy land.

SAMURAI WARLORDS
The samurai were the military elite of Japan, rather like the medieval knights of Europe. Their military power and political skills enabled them to control local governments and land. Samurai clans were in a continual state of civil war until 1603, when they all came under the ruling dynasty of Tokugawa Ieyasu.

NAPOLEONIC WARS
Napoleon was one of the greatest commanders in history and redrew the map of Europe between 1799 and 1815. The Frenchman had ambitious plans to conquer the whole of Europe and Russia as well. This led to a 15-year period of turmoil and battles around Europe, from Spain to Russia.

Japan

Mounted samurai warriors ride out from Himeji Castle (below)

SAMURAI CASTLES

Samurai castles were situated to guard the routes connecting the *daimyo* (warlord) territories with hostile neighbouring lands. If a site lacked strong natural defences, artificial barriers such as moats and walls were built. Between 1570 and 1690 was the golden age of Japanese castle construction.

SHOGUNS AND SAMURAI

HIMEJI CASTLE

The castle (above and below) was completed in 1609. This beautiful structure is covered in intricately carved and painted woodwork. Other features included multiple gateways, courtyards, reception halls, watchtowers, stables and workshops.

The samurai were the warrior class who served local lords in medieval Japan. Military families dominated Japan from around the 12th century, after the emperor had been replaced by a military overlord, called a *shogun*. There followed many years of turmoil, with continual outbreaks of fighting between rival lords. Throughout these years of unrest, the samurai followed the code of *bushido* (the way of the warrior). The basis of this code was unquestioning loyalty to one's lord. This bond of service was often so strong that if their lord died in battle his followers might commit mass suicide rather than surrender or serve another leader.

The Battle of Sekigahara, on 21st October, 1600, was the most decisive in the history of Japan. Ishida Mitsunari (with 100,000 troops) and Tokugawa Ieyasu (with 75,000) fought to be master of Japan. After a fierce hand-to-hand battle, 30,000 men lay dead. Ieyasu had won and three years later was given the title of Shogun.

a   b   c   d   e   f   g

TYPES OF SAMURAI WARRIORS

(a) An archer's 'kyudo' bamboo bow could be shot from horseback or standing.

(b) An *arquebusier* was a samurai with a type of musket.

(c) A spearman carried spears up to 4.5 m long.

(d) A standard-bearer.

(e) An army commander wore full metal armour and a *kabuto* (crested helmet).

(f) Bodyguard with a *daito* (long sword).

(g) Low-class *bushi* (foot soldier) armed with a *nagamaki* (a kind of slashing spear, with a long wooden handle and a sword-like blade).

ARMOUR

Elaborate samurai armour (below) was made from lacquered iron and leather segments held together with silk cords. The sleeves and legs were made from chain mail and helmets often had crests and iron face masks. Attached to their backs were colourful banners with their clan's crest on them.

Head detail from a samurai suit of armour

ENGLISH CIVIL WAR

Conflict arose between Charles I of England and Parliament over how to deal with Scotland and Ireland. The King was causing religious unrest in both of these countries by enforcing Protestant rule. Charles needed money from taxes to do this, but Parliament refused to help him and demanded that he dismiss some of his most senior aides whom they distrusted. When Charles attempted to arrest five troublesome Members of Parliament on 4th January, 1642, many people were angered and riots broke out in London. The King was forced to flee the city. By October the King had raised an army of 13,000 men and headed toward London. The Parliamentary troops left the capital to cut him off, under the leadership of the Earl of Essex. The forces first met at Edgehill (23rd October, 1642) and the King narrowly won this battle, but later retreated to establish headquarters in Oxford. Though at first the Royalists had success in much of England, especially in the south west (capturing Bristol on 26th July, 1643), Charles still did not advance on London.

A 'mortuary hilt' sword, as used by cavalry soldiers during the Civil War

MAJOR BATTLES

The map above shows the principal battles between the Royalists (Cavaliers) and the Parliamentarians (Roundheads).

A 19th-century painting of the Battle of Marston Moor, 1644 (below)

MARSTON MOOR, 2ND JULY, 1644

Under Leslie, First Earl of Leven, the Scots came south and joined with the Parliamentary forces. At the Battle of Marston Moor (below), near York, these forces crushed the Royalists led by Prince Rupert – the King's nephew and the Duke of Newcastle. York now surrendered to the Parliamentarian army and the Scots stormed Newcastle on 19th October with 21,000 men.

New Model Army

In the winter of 1644-45 the British Parliament suffered heavy defeats and was having problems with its army regarding pay. The solution was to bring together old army units under the leadership of commanders Sir Thomas Fairfax and Oliver Cromwell. This was known as the 'New Model Army', consisting of 22,000 full-time, paid and trained men. This army met and defeated the Royalists at Naseby on 14th June, 1645, and by May of 1646 the King was under siege at Oxford. The Civil War officially ended when Oxford surrendered to Parliament on 24th June, but the King escaped from the city in disguise and gave himself up to the Scots. At first the Scots would not help Charles, because he would not agree to their demands. Having again escaped Cromwell's clutches, Charles eventually persuaded the Scots to help him, but their army was defeated by Cromwell and Fairfax at the Battle of Preston in 1648. The King was taken under arrest to Windsor and after a vote in Parliament, King Charles was made to stand trial as a traitor to his country. He was sentenced to death and executed by having his head cut off.

ARTILLERY
The heavy artillery of an army was stationed at the rear, where it could fire over the heads of the infantry.

Smaller cannons (left), that fired nails and scrap iron in canvas bags, were positioned in front of the infantry.

Re-creation of a small cannon used in the English Civil War

Helmet

Leather tunic

Short-barrelled musket

Red sashes were worn by Roundheads early in the war to identify themselves in battle

CAVALRYMEN
These soldiers carried a sword and a short-barrelled musket. The main strategy was to advance at a quick trot until in range of the enemy. The men in the front fired, then wheeled away. In their second charge they advanced at a gallop using their swords.

THE DEATH OF A KING

After a week-long trial, King Charles I was executed on 30th January, 1649 (above). Before his head was cut off, his final words were, "I am a martyr to the people". Oliver Cromwell had signed the King's death warrant himself.

Re-creation of pikemen from the English Civil War

PIKEMEN

Pikemen (above) were foot soldiers armed with 5-m-long pointed pikes. They stood at the centre of battle formations to keep advancing enemy cavalry at bay. Well-disciplined pikemen, brave enough to hold their ground, could do tremendous damage to cavalry charging straight at them.

TYRANT OR SAVIOUR?

After the execution of Charles I, Oliver Cromwell brutally suppressed uprisings in both Scotland and Ireland. A new Parliament was formed, consisting of 140 'godly' (religious) men who made Cromwell Lord Protector (temporary Head of State). His first act was to make a peace treaty with the Dutch in 1654, which ended years of trade wars and helped the British Empire expand overseas.

Death mask of Oliver Cromwell (right), made by taking a wax impression of his face at the time of his death

WAR OF THE SPANISH SUCCESSION, 1701-14

At the end of the 17th century the king of Spain, Charles II, died without an heir. All of Europe contested for the vast territories owned by the Habsburg family, which included large parts of Europe and lands in the Americas. It soon became a struggle between the two most powerful families in Europe, the Habsburgs under Leopold I and the Bourbons under Louis XIV. Fearing that one nation might become too powerful, the British and their Dutch allies sided with Leopold I to stop the French from becoming a European superpower.

JOHN CHURCHILL, DUKE OF MARLBOROUGH

During the war, English commander Marlborough (right) waged ten successful campaigns, besieged over thirty towns, and never lost a battle or skirmish.

Duke of Marlborough

CHAIN OF COMMAND

Marlborough's army was well organised. He relayed messages through 'aides-de-camp' (below) – foot-runners who acted as his eyes and ears on the battlefield.

Aide-de-camp

In 1702, the duke of Marlborough joined forces with Prince Eugene of Savoy to prevent the French from advancing on Vienna, Austria. The armies fought near the German village of Blenheim in August 1704, where the French and German forces lost around 30,000 men. Later in the war, in 1708, Marlborough scored a decisive victory over the French duke of Vendome at the battle of Oudenarde. Following this victory, the war was brought to a conclusion as the British and Dutch forces overwhelmed their enemies over the next few years.

Sword

Long coat

The French army of Louis XIV (above) had long coats, waistcoats, pants, and stockings. Each carried a sword and flintlock musket with a bayonet. Sergeants wore cuffs edged with gold lace.

DRAGONS
DE MONSÈIGNEUR LE DUC
DE PENTHIEVRE,
En Garnifon à Quimper, en Bretagné.

PROPAGANDA
Recruiting poster (above) for the dragoons of the duke of Vendome, who was also known as the duke of Penthievre. Dragoons were heavily armed mounted military troops.

Flintlock musket with bayonet

Cannon

Drum

FREDERICK THE GREAT

Frederick the Great of Prussia (part of modern Germany and Poland) had a well-trained army. He used it to great effect when he invaded the Austrian-ruled land of Silesia (part of present-day Poland) on December 16th, 1740. The Austrians, weakened by a recent war with the Ottomans, were not expecting the attack, and so the province quickly fell.

In 1741, Frederick invaded Bohemia (in the present-day Czech Republic), capturing Prague after a short siege.

In 1745, the Austrians, under Charles of Lorraine, were determined to drive the

Musket with bayonet

Prussians from Silesia but were out-maneuvered by Frederick's well-drilled infantry and cavalry. These victories forced the Austrians to accept the Prussian claim to Silesia at the Peace of Dresden. Due to the rise of Prussia, Russia and Austria allied themselves to crush their expanding enemy. Between 1756 and 1763, most of Europe was at war. France sided with Russia and Austria, while Britain, Sweden, and Germany allied themselves with Prussia. Finally, in 1762, a Russo-Prussian peace was ordered by Peter III of Russia, and hostilities ceased. The Austrians followed suit on February 15th, 1763.

A GREAT LEADER
Frederick II (left) spent his childhood in rigorous military training and education. As an adult, he studied music and French literature. He directed the internal affairs of his country with passion and prudence. By the time he died, he had nearly doubled the area of the Prussian kingdom.

PRUSSIAN INFANTRY
Frederick the Great's army was well-paid and well-equipped. It had grown to 154,000 men by 1756. His army was adept at drills and discipline, and in time could move into position flawlessly to execute complex tactics. The Prussian infantry carried flintlock muskets with bayonets.

Marching gaiters

This image (left) depicts soldiers in red, yellow and white uniforms. It is from a 1789 publication entitled *Preussische Armee Uniformen unter Friedrich Wilhelm II*, meaning "Prussian Army Uniforms under Frederick William II."

A BRAVE LEADER
Twice, Frederick was wounded on the battlefield when the horse he was riding was shot. He is pictured below with two of the 5th Hussars (a unit of light cavalry soldiers).

Frederick the Great

Hussar

BATTLES FOR INDEPENDENCE

*I*n the Autumn of 1775, the Americans invaded Canada in an attempt to cut off the British soldiers in New England. After a six-week siege, Fort St. Jean surrendered, as did the forces at Fort Chambly and Montreal. In 1777, the British tried to cut the thirteen colonies in half. They won victories at Brandywine and Germantown, but the strategy failed after battles at Bemis Heights and Bennington. With the arrival of the French in 1778, the power balance shifted, and the British moved south. The end of the war came with the Battle of Yorktown, Virginia, in 1781 (below). The British force, under General Cornwallis, was surrounded by the forces of Washington (American) and Rochambeau (French). America had finally won its independence.

Map (above) showing the major battles of the American War of Independence, from Bunker Hill to the British surrender at Yorktown in 1781

An 18th-century oil painting depicting British troops attacking the Americans at the Battle of Bunker Hill

An 18th-century colored engraving depicting the British surrendering to George Washington after their defeat at Yorktown

BUNKER HILL, JUNE 17TH, 1775

The first major battle of the war took place at Bunker Hill (above). The Americans, who were entrenched on top of the hill, inflicted heavy casualties on the British lines of infantry. However, when the Americans ran out of ammunition, the British eventually drove them back.

BRITISH SURRENDER

Besieged at Yorktown, Cornwallis and the British troops sustained heavy bombardment for 14 days. British ships bringing more troops to relieve Yorktown were blocked at Virginia Capes by the French Navy under Admiral De Grasse. Under constant fire and with no sign of relief, Cornwallis surrendered (above).

Continentals bombarding Yorktown with artillery

NAPOLEONIC WARS, 1797-1815

Napoleon Bonaparte

Napoleon rose out of the chaos of the violent revolution in France (1787-1799), in which the king, queen, and thousands of others were executed. Born in Corsica in 1769, the young Napoleon was sent to French military school and graduated to become a lieutenant in the artillery. By 1796, he had taken command of the French army in Italy to counter the threat of an Austrian invasion. Within a year, he had driven them out. He fought with new tactics, often marching at night, attacking in the rain, and even fighting on Sundays, which had been unheard of before). Napoleon next attacked Egypt to disrupt the British trade routes there. At first he was successful. He won the Battle of Cairo on July 21st, 1798 and defeated the Egyptian Mamelukes army at Giza, capturing Suez. However, at the Battle of the Nile on August 1st, 1798, the French fleet was destroyed. They lost six ships (four sunk, two captured) to British Admiral Nelson.

Bearskin helmet

Cartridge box

Flintlock musket

Recreation of soldiers from the
Napoleonic Imperial Guard

SHAKO PLATE

Worn on the front of a soldier's helmet, the shako plate (above) was decorated with the symbol of an eagle and marked with the maxim of the French Republic: "Liberté, Egalité, Fraternité" (Freedom, Equality, Brotherhood).

Hussar

Polish Lancer

Dragoon

UNIFORMS

The Napoleonic era was a "golden age" of military uniforms (above and right), which were as grand as possible, both to impress the enemy and to raise the morale of the wearer. Unfortunately, these fancy uniforms were usually impractical.

NELSON'S NAVY

It has been said that all that separated Britain from an invasion by Napoleon were the ships of the British Navy (nicknamed the "Wooden Walls"). In 1789, there were around 16,000 officers and men in naval service. By 1803, this number had risen to 120,000 because of the war with France. At this time, the Navy had over 110 warships that used to defend the country, attack enemy navies, control distant colonies, and protect merchant ships. Britain's strong sea power made the country one of the most powerful nations in the world during this period.

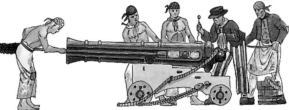

Captain

Lieutenant

NELSON (1758-1805)
Horatio Nelson rose rapidly through the ranks to become a captain at the age of 21. His bold leadership brought him decisive victories at the Nile (1798) and Copenhagen (1801). His most famous victory at the Battle of Trafalgar (1805) cost him his life.

MEMBERS OF THE CREW
The crew of a ship like the *Victory* was enormous: 600 strong, including 150 marines, as well as 20 officers, lieutenants, and the captain.

Midshipman (with a speaking trumpet)

"Powder monkey"– a man who supplied the gunners with gunpowder

Horatio Nelson

Gun crews (above) worked quickly on deck. It took an experienced crew two to five minutes to clean, load, aim, and fire a cannon.

VARIOUS AMMUNITION
There were different types of projectiles used for different purposes, such as to cut down sails and rigging, to kill enemy soldiers, and to penetrate the wooden hulls of enemy ships.

Various types of ammunition

HMS VICTORY

Nelson's flagship, the *HMS Victory* (below), was built between 1759-1765 using 2,000 oak trees. The *Victory* was a "first rate" ship, meaning it had over 100. These were distributed along four gun decks on each side of the ship.

HMS Victory

Detail from the HMS Victory

Gun ports

Large ships like the Victory were difficult to handle. It had 32 diffrent sails and about 24 miles of rigging.

CROSSING THE LINE

Tactics were to "cross the line" (right) of enemy fleets to separate them into smaller units and enable all guns to fire at once on a target.

Diagram showing how a ship would "cross the line"

BATTLE OF TRAFALGAR, 1805

In 1805, Napoleon planned to invade Britain. He ordered Admiral Villeneuve's combined Franco-Spanish fleet to make a diversionary voyage, before returning to cover the invasion. Nelson chased this  fleet back to Spain and the invasion plan was abandoned. The Franco-Spanish fleet then sailed to support French forces in the Mediterranean. Nelson's fleet of 27 ships intercepted it at Cape Trafalgar (off the Spanish coast) on October 21st and after an epic sea battle (above), 19 of Napoleon's 33 ships surrendered or were destroyed.

PENINSULAR WARS

In 1804, Napoleon appointed himself emperor of France. In the following years he had great military successes, first against the Russians and Austrians at Austerlitz and later against the Prussians in a series of lightning attacks. In 1807, Napoleon enforced a blockade of British trade. He did this by invading Spain and Portugal, where he installed his cousin, Joseph Bonaparte, as king. British General Sir Arthur Wellesly landed a small army in Portugal to drive the French out and the Peninsular Wars began. Although Wellesly won initial battles at Rolica and Vimiero, the British were forced to retreat to Corunna for the winter. Wellesly then advanced rapidly and drove the French out of Portugal. In 1810, the French, under Marshal Massena, invaded Spain and Portugal once more but were defeated at Fuentes d'Onoro (1811) and Salamanca (1812). After five years of bloody conflict, the Peninsular Wars ended in 1813, when the French evacuated Madrid. It signalled an end to the French domination of Europe.

Map showing the Spanish peninsula and the major battles of the campaign

THE BATTLE OF SALAMANCA
This was a decisive blow to Napoleon's grip on the Spanish peninsula. More than 7,000 French troops were killed, and a further 7,000 were captured, when they tried to attack the Duke of Wellington's army near Salamanca (below).

Captured French troops being led into Salamanca (below)

30

A flintlock pistol from the Napoleonic era

As well as a sabre, French cavalry troops would have carried a pistol (above)

Peaked helmet

Curved sword

Decorative tassles in the hussar style

ARTHUR WELLESLY, DUKE OF WELLINGTON

Known as "The Iron Duke" by his soldiers, Wellesly (above) was born in Ireland and joined the British army in 1787. In 1796, he was sent to India and became a prominent soldier and administrator. On his return to Britain, he was knighted. He took command of the British forces against Napoleon in the Peninsular Wars and was made duke of Wellington in 1814.

CAVALRY

Troops on horseback were divided into heavy and light units. Heavy cavalry were used for shock tactics and would try to smash through the enemy line by brute force. The light cavalry (right), used mostly for flanking maneuvers and pursuit, wore no armor and carried curved swords for slashing. Massed for the attack, they were an imposing sight. Walking slowly towards the enemy's troops, they patiently waited for the signal to charge as gun shot and shell rained down on them.

Recreation of a member of the British light dragoons

CRIMEAN WAR, 1854-1856

When Russia marched into Ottoman territories across the River Danube in March 1854, both Britain and France were concerned. Britain was fearful that Russia would threaten British trade with India. The new leader of France, Napoleon III, was worried about French interests in that area. So, on March 28th, 1854, Britain and France declared war on Russia. The allied forces, led by Lord Ragland (British) and Marshal St. Arnaud (French), reached the Black Sea in August, 1854. On September 14th, the allies landed at Eupatoria on the Crimean coast. The inferior Russian forces were defeated at the Alma River on September 20th, at Balaclava on October 25th, and at Inkerman on November 5th. After a year-long siege, the Russian naval base at Sevastopol surrendered to the allies on September 10th, 1855. The new Russian Tsar, Alexander II, signed a surrender in Paris on March 30th, 1856. This ended the war and secured the neutrality of the Black Sea.

CHARGE OF THE LIGHT BRIGADE
The Charge of the Light Brigade (below) at Balaclava was one of Britain's most notorious military actions. As a result of confusion over some orders, a brigade of light cavalry were ordered to charge down a narrow valley 1.5 miles long, straight at thirty Russian cannon with batteries on either side. One of the cavalry regiments was the 17th Lancers (below).

A bugle used in the charge of the Light Brigade

HOSPITALS

The medical conditions for men who were injured in battle were appalling. After reports of the terrible sanitation in a hospital in Scutari, Turkey, appeared in the newspapers, a woman called Florence  Nightingale (left) obtained permission to take nurses to the Crimea to clean up the hospital. When she arrived on November 7th, 1854, doctors refused to help her until they became overloaded with wounded men from the Battle of Inkerman. At that time, up to 42 percent of admitted casualties died in the rat-infested hospital. With Nightingale's strict regime of cleanliness and the nurses' efforts, this was cut to 2 percent.

Map showing the major battles of the Crimean War (above)

Shako helmet

Lance

Blue double-breasted uniform

Cartridge box

A MASSACRE

Out of the 607 brigadiers who rode out in the Charge of the Light Brigade, only 198 returned. Although the brave and risky charge had no military value, the British won the battle against a much stronger Russian force.

Recreation of a member of the Light Brigade

THE UNION VICTORY

The first major battle of the American Civil War proved that there would be no easy victory for the Union troops. They were driven back when they tried to break through Confederate lines at Bull Run, Virginia. Later in the war, their superior numbers and better equipment set them ahead in the war. The Confederates repeatedly attempted to rally and fight back, but they spent a great deal of time in retreat. In the Battle of Gettysburg in July 1863, they suffered overwhelming casualties. The Confederate commander, General Lee, was forced to surrender his last 7,800 troops on April 9th, 1865, at Appomattox in Virginia.

ULYSSES S. GRANT
Grant (1822-1885), seated third from left in the photo above, entered the war as a colonel of volunteers in support of the Union and was rapidly promoted. He was later President of the U.S. from 1867 to 1877.

ARTILLERY

The war saw a progressive transition from smooth-bore to rifled field guns by both sides.

GUNSHIPS

Floating mortar vessels had no engines but could heavily bombard enemy positions on land.

TRAINS

The Union used trains to move men, supplies, and artillery to needed locations. This gave them an advantage.

IRONCLADS

These new, heavily-armored warships were almost indestructible. When the *Merrimac* (Confederate) and the *Monitor* (Union) met in battle on March 9th, 1862, the battle raged for four hours before being called off, because the men were exhausted from loading the cannon.

The Union army attacking at Gettysburg

ROBERT E. LEE

Lee (1807-1870, left) was the leading Confederate general. He became the military advisor to the President of the Southern Confederacy, Jefferson Davis. In 1862, he commanded the Northern Army in victories at Fredericksburg and Chancellorsville. He was a great commander and sometimes defeated larger Union armies with his superior tactics.

AMERICAN INDIAN WARS, 1854-90

A colt revolver as used in the "Wild West"

In the mid 1800s, a great stream of pioneers, ranchers, and gold panners poured into the "Wild West." They brought with them diseases like smallpox, which wiped out whole tribes of Native Americans. White hunters slaughtered millions of buffalo, and farmers fenced off the huge open plains. One by one, the tribes were forced off their land and onto reservations by the U.S. government. Most went peacefully, but others chose to fight. The most famous victory was at the Battle of the Little Big Horn. But the Native American tribes could never entirely defeat the larger and more powerful U.S. army. The soldiers burnt their villages and showed no mercy. By 1890, no Plains Indians remained free.

GENERAL GEORGE CUSTER
Called "Long Hair" by the Native Americans, Custer (above) was in command of the 7th Cavalry. He had served in the Civil War on the Union side. He attacked Chief Sitting Bull's huge camp at the Little Big Horn in 1876, but Custer's men were defeated and all 265 men were killed.

General

Captain

Cavalryman   *Native American scout*

INSIDE A FORT
Each captain was in charge of a company of 25 men. A sergeant kept discipline and gave day-to-day orders. Senior officers, such as generals and colonels, would visit the fort to pass on government orders, negotiate treaties with the Indians, or organize attacks against them. Cavalrymen carried sabres, revolvers, and rifles. Native American scouts were used to find camps or guide soldiers along trails.

FORT LARAMIE
Fort Laramie (right), Wyoming, was a post thriving with trappers, miners, Native Americans, and pioneers on their way westwards. Later, during the Indian Wars, the U.S. army built forts all over the West, and Fort Laramie became a military complex.

*Recreation of a
Native American fighter*

War paint

*Bone
breastplate*

Rifle and case

Moccasins

*Native American
rider's gauntlets*

NATIVE WARRIORS
Native American warriors, like this Cheyenne
(left), fought on horseback. They wore war paint to
make themselves look fierce. Their weapons' cases
for guns and bows had decorative bead work, as did
their moccasins. They wore a breastplate made out
of bone and carried a shield to protect themselves.

Bow

Shield

SITTING BULL
A warrior and medicine man,
Sitting Bull was the most
famous of all the Sioux Indians.
Along with other chiefs, he led
his warriors in a war against
men who were trying to drive
Native Americans onto
reservations. After Little Big
Horn, he fled to Canada but
eventually surrendered.

NATIVE AMERICAN TACTICS
The tribes often used hit-and-run
tactics (below), avoiding open
battles where they would be
out-gunned. They often laid
ambushes, drawing soldiers into a
trap by using a small group of
warriors as bait.

TIME LINE

American War of Independence

1550-1650
Warring feudal nobles with samurai armies fight over territories in Japan.

1587
Francis Drake makes an expedition to Cadiz and destroys 33 Spanish ships.

English warship

1588
The Spanish Armada attacks England and is repelled by English ships.

1642-1646
The English Civil War. King Charles I is beheaded in 1649.

1652
Following the *Navigations Act* (1651), England and the Netherlands are at war over control of sea routes and regulation of colonial trade.

1658
At the Battle of the Dunes, an Anglo-French alliance defeats the Spanish army.

1688
The "Glorious Revolution" in Britain. King James II is overthrown, and William of Orange is crowned King of Britain. In 1690, at the Battle of the Boyne, James is defeated in Ireland by William III (formerly William of Orange).

1701-1714
The War of the Spanish Succession. In the Battle of Blenheim (1704), the British and Prince Eugene of Savoy destroy a Franco-Bavarian force. In 1708, they defeat the French at Oudenarde.

1701
The Kingdom of Prussia is established.

1707
Scotland is formally joined with England and Wales to form the United Kingdom.

1745
The Jacobite rebellion. "Bonnie Prince Charlie" enters a conflict with George I over the right to the British throne and is defeated at the Battle of Culloden (1746).

1756-1763
The Seven Years' War was fought between Russia, Austria, and France against the expansion of Prussian power. Frederick II of Prussia defeats the Austrians at Prague in 1757. At the Battle of Zorndorf (1758), Frederick wins and ends the Russian threat. He is defeated by a Austro-Russian force at Kunersdorf in 1759. In 1763, the Treaty of Hubertusburg ends the Seven Years' War, after Tsar Peter III of Russia begins peace talks.

1761-1762
The Spanish try to invade Portugal but are driven back.

1775-1783
The American War of Independence. The first shots are fired at Lexington. George Washington takes command of the Continental Army. After a siege, the British abandon Boston. France and Spain give support to the American side. The Battle of Bemis Heights, Saratoga, is an American victory and the turning point in the war. In 1781, the Americans besiege Yorktown, and British General Cornwallis surrenders.

1782
Britain signs the Treaty of Paris, recognizing U.S. independence.

1797-1815
The Napoleonic Wars. French Emperor Napoleon's Egyptian expedition defeats the Egyptian Mamelukes at Cairo, and the French fleet is almost destroyed by Nelson.

1800
Napoleon crosses the Alps into Italy.

1805
British Admiral Nelson wins at the Battle of Trafalgar but loses

Battle of Trafalgar

his life to a French sniper. Napoleon wins battles at Ulm and Austerlitz.

1806
Napoleon wins at Jena, enters Berlin, and carries on to Warsaw.

1808
Napoleon starts his Spanish campaign.

1809
The French win the Battle of Wagram against the Austrians.

1812-1813
Napoleon attacks Russia and marches to Moscow to find the city in flames. He retreats and his army lose more than 300,000 men in the winter conditions.

1814
While Napoleon resists invasion by Russia, Austria, and Prussia, the British Duke of Wellington advances into France from Spain and takes Toulouse. Meanwhile, Paris is taken by the eastern allies. Napoleon goes into exile on the island of Elba.

Napoleon Bonaparte

1815
Napoleon escapes from Elba and returns to France. He meets Wellington's army at Waterloo and is defeated after the late arrival of the Prussians.

1854-1856
The Crimean War. French, British, and Ottoman Turks fight against the Russians' invasion of the Turkish-controlled Christian holy land.

1854
Allied forces defeat the Russians at Alma, Balaclava, and Inkerman.

1855
France and Britain capture Sevastopol after a yearlong siege.

1856
Peace treaty signed at Paris ends the Crimean War.

1861
The American Civil War begins. Southerners shell Union-held Fort Sumter in South Carolina. Union forces advance on the southern capital, Richmond.

1863
Confederate General Lee loses the Battle at Gettysburg with 31,000 casualties.

1864
Union General Grant invades the South with a larger and better equipped army. Lee's Northern Army is pinned down defending Petersburg and Richmond.

1865
On April 9th, General Lee is forced to surrender at Appomattox, Virginia, ending

the war. On April 14th, President Lincoln is assassinated.

1854
The American Indian Wars begin.

1862
Little Crow the Younger leads a Sioux uprising.

1870
The Franco-Prussian War lasts 44 days. Napoleon III of France surrenders on September 2nd at Sedan to Kaiser William.

1874
Colonel Mackenzie defeats the Comanches at Red River.

1876
Chief Sitting Bull unifies the Sioux and defeats General Custer at the Battle of the Little Big Horn.

American Indian Wars

1877
The famous Native warrior Crazy Horse is killed at Fort Robinson, Nebraska.

1889
Geronimo surrenders.

1890
The Battle of Wounded Knee. The final battle of the American Indian Wars occurs.

GLOSSARY

Armada A large number of ships.

Artillery High caliber guns.

Bandolier A soldier's shoulder belt with small pockets or loops for gun cartridges.

Battery An artillery unit.

Bayonet A blade attached to a gun used for close combat fighting.

Cache A store of weapons.

Cartridges Ammunition for firearms.

Casualty A soldier killed or wounded in enemy action.

Cavalier A supporter of King Charles I during the English Civil War.

Cavalry Troops who fight on horseback.

Clan A group of families with a common ancestor.

Colony A territory occupied and ruled by a foreign state.

Confederacy The southern states which fought the Union in the American Civil War.

Continental The name given to the British who fought to keep the 13 northern states in the American War of Independence.

Drill Training in military procedures.

Empire Territory under the rule of a sovereign state.

Exile A forced absence from one's home or country.

Expansionism The policy of expanding the territory of a country.

Gold panner Someone searching for gold.

Grenade An explosive thrown by hand.

Infantry Soldiers who fight on foot.

Ironclad A warship with iron plating.

Jacobite A Scottish follower of James II.

Moccasins Soft leather shoes.

Morale The spirit of optimism within a group or individual.

Ottoman Empire The Turkish empire.

Privateer A privately owned ship authorized by government.

Redcoat A type of British soldier.

Reservation An area of land set aside for American Indians.

Revolver A pistol with a cylindrical chamber.

Roundhead A supporter of Parliament during the English Civil War.

Royalist A supporter of the ruling monarch.

Saber A type of sword with a curved blade.

Samurai A Japanese warrior.

Shogun A Japanese military commander.

Smallpox A highly contagious disease.

Sniper A concealed rifleman.

Speaking trumpet An instrument that makes the speaker's voice louder.

Succession When the leadership of a nation passes from one person to another.

Tactics Military maneuvers to outwit an enemy.

Taxes A compulsory payment issued to the government.

Treaty An agreement between nations or states.

Uniform Clothing that identifies which side of a battle a soldier belongs to.

Union The northern states in the American Civil War.

Volunteer A person who serves their country willingly.

INDEX

Page numbers in **bold** refer to illustrations.